UNWRAPPED
MARVELOUS
MUMMIES

MODERN MUMMIES

by Joyce Markovics

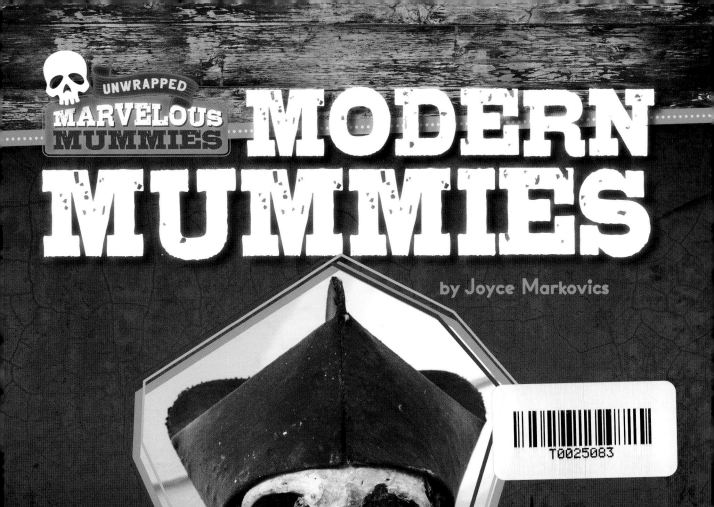

T0025083

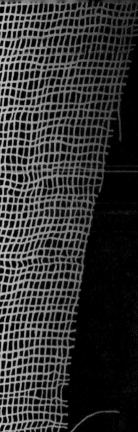

CHERRY LAKE PRESS

Published in the United States of America by Cherry Lake Publishing Group
Ann Arbor, Michigan
www.cherrylakepublishing.com

Reading Adviser: Marla Conn, MS Ed., Literacy specialist, Read-Ability, Inc.
Content Adviser: Owen Beattie, PhD
Book Designer: Ed Morgan

Photo Credits: © Lucky Team Studio/Shutterstock, cover and title page; Wikimedia Commons, TOC; © duchy/Shutterstock, 4; Wikimedia Commons, 5 top; freepik.com, 5 bottom; Wikimedia Commons, 6; © Gandolfo Cannatella/Shutterstock, 7; © Stefano cellai/Shutterstock, 8; © Katarzyna Uroda/Shutterstock, 9 top; © Diego Fiore/Shutterstock, 9 bottom; © Diego Fiore/Shutterstock, 10 top; Wikimedia Commons, 10 bottom; Wikimedia Commons, 11; © Tyler Olson/Shutterstock, 12–13; © GUDKOV ANDRET/Shutterstock, 13; © National Geographic Image Collection/Alamy Stock Photo, 14; © Robbie Fatt/Shutterstock, 15; Wikimedia Commons, 16; © SPUTNIK/Alamy Stock Photo, 17; Wikimedia Commons, 18 top; Wikimedia Commons, 18 bottom; Wikimedia Commons, 19; Wikimedia Commons, 20; Library of Congress, 21.

Copyright © 2021 by Cherry Lake Publishing Group
All rights reserved. No part of this book may be reproduced or utilized in any form or by any means without written permission from the publisher.

Cherry Lake Press is an imprint of Cherry Lake Publishing Group.

Library of Congress Cataloging-in-Publication Data
Names: Markovics, Joyce L., author.
Title: Modern mummies / by Joyce L. Markovics.
Description: Ann Arbor, Michigan : Cherry Lake Publishing, [2021] | Series:
    Unwrapped: marvelous mummies | Includes bibliographical references and
    index. | Audience: Ages 8 | Audience: Grades 2-3
Identifiers: LCCN 2020030264 (print) | LCCN 2020030265 (ebook) | ISBN
    9781534180444 (hardcover) | ISBN 9781534182158 (paperback) | ISBN
    9781534183162 (ebook) | ISBN 9781534181458 (pdf)
Subjects: LCSH: Mummies—Juvenile literature.
Classification: LCC GN293 .M355 2021 (print) | LCC GN293 (ebook) | DDC
    599.9—dc23
LC record available at https://lccn.loc.gov/2020030264
LC ebook record available at https://lccn.loc.gov/2020030265

Printed in the United States of America
Corporate Graphics

CONTENTS

SLEEPING BEAUTY

In 1920, Rosalia Lombardo died of the flu in Palermo, Sicily. She was only 2 years old at the time. Her parents were overcome with grief. They asked an embalmer named Alfredo Salafia to preserve their daughter's body. Alfredo was a master mummy maker!

Palermo, Sicily

When Alfredo finished embalming Rosalia's body, the Lombardos were shocked. Their dead daughter looked as if she were peacefully sleeping. Her mummified body became known as Sleeping Beauty.

ROSALIA LOMBARDO
Nata 1918—Morta 1920

Rosalia's embalmed body

Sicily is a large island. It's located off the southern tip of Italy.

5

Rosalia's mummy was placed in the Capuchin (kah-POO-chin) catacombs for all to see. The Capuchins are an all-male religious group that formed in 1534. For years, the monks buried their dead in a large underground area.

Rosalia's body is still in the Capuchin catacombs today. It was placed in a special case to further preserve it.

At first, only dead monks were buried in the catacombs. Then the Capuchins allowed wealthy people, like Rosalia's parents, to bury family members there. Relatives paid to have the bodies cared for. Sometimes, the monks would even change the mummies' clothing! Today, over 1,200 mummies can be found in the Capuchin catacombs.

The Capuchins believed that mummies were holy and should be on display.

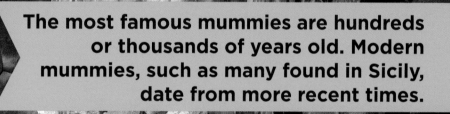

The most famous mummies are hundreds or thousands of years old. Modern mummies, such as many found in Sicily, date from more recent times.

ITALIAN MUMMY MAKERS

Typically, when a person dies, bacteria and chemicals break down the flesh. This process is called decomposition. A mummy is a dead body that has not totally decomposed. It may still have bits of skin or other flesh.

This mummy still has most of its skin.

Mummies can either form naturally or through an artificial process. Most of the mummies in the Capuchin catacombs formed naturally. How? Sicily is very hot and dry. The dead bodies quickly dried up. This stopped the growth of bacteria and slowed decomposition.

A naturally formed mummy

Sicily is home to thousands of mummies. In the 1990s, a secret tomb filled with mummies was found at a church in Novara di Sicilia.

9

The Capuchins also used other methods to preserve the dead. Sometimes, they bathed bodies in a toxic chemical. The chemical, called arsenic, helped preserve the flesh.

An old glass bottle containing the chemical arsenic

LIQ. ARSENICAL.

This illustration shows embalmers examining a dead body.

A more effective way to preserve the dead is through embalming. This process uses a combination of chemicals. It not only preserves the body, it can make the dead appear lifelike! Alfredo Salafia perfected this method with Rosalia. She's said to be the "world's most beautiful mummy."

Tools and supplies used for embalming a body

Alfredo Salafia was a self-taught embalmer. He preserved over 100 bodies—even his own brother!

SMOKED BODIES

The Italians aren't the only modern mummy makers. In Papua New Guinea, the Anga people created smoked mummies. First, they built a special shelter called a smoking hut. They placed the dead body in the hut and started a fire. The fire produced a lot of smoke.

These huts in Papua New Guinea are similar to ones used by the Anga people.

Over 30 days, the Anga tended the fire and smoked the body. During this time, they scraped and squeezed it to draw out fluids. Finally, the dried body was covered in red clay. This helped draw out any extra fluids.

The completed mummy was placed in a chair on a cliff for all to see!

Smoking is another way to preserve flesh.

son, Gematsu, wants to bring back the tradition. For the Anga, it's a great honor to be mummified.

Chief Moimango's mummy and Gematsu (*back left*)

14

Until then, Gematsu and his people tend to their mummies. Some have cracks or peeling skin. The Anga use materials from the forest to patch the bodies. Tree sap is used as glue. Rope and clay are used to hold the mummies together.

A mummy in need of preservation

When Gematsu dies, he hopes to become a mummy!

FAMOUS MUMMIES

Several famous modern-day people have also been mummified. Russian leader Vladimir Lenin started a revolution. When he died in 1924, his body was embalmed for "all eternity."

Lenin's mummy has been on display since he died. The body was placed inside a very large tomb called a mausoleum. Tens of millions of people have visited Lenin's body over the years.

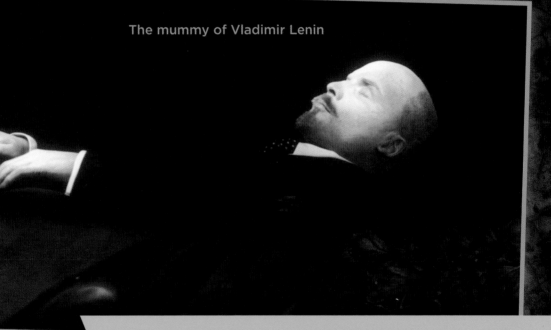

The mummy of Vladimir Lenin

To help preserve it, embalmers treat Lenin's body with chemicals every 18 months.

Jeremy Bentham was an English philosopher. He believed in helping people lead better lives. Before he died in 1832 at age 84, he asked that his body be preserved. His own body, he decided, would be his memorial.

A painting of Jeremy Bentham

Jeremy Bentham's dead body before it was cut open

Jeremy Bentham called his mummy "auto-icon," or self-image.

Doctors removed Bentham's insides as people watched. Then the doctors mummified his head. His skeleton was dressed in his own clothes. Finally, his head and skeleton were put on display in London, England!

Abraham Lincoln was one of America's greatest presidents. In 1865, he was shot and killed at the age of 56. His body was embalmed. Then his mummy was carried by train from Washington, D.C., to his hometown in Springfield, Illinois, to be buried.

The train carrying Abraham Lincoln's body

Along the way, the train stopped at many cities. Americans saw Lincoln's mummy and paid their respects. His face looked so lifelike some people reached out to touch it! After Lincoln, many Americans wanted to be embalmed too.

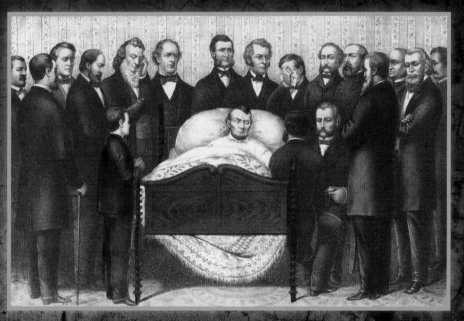

The dead body of Abraham Lincoln

Lincoln's body was taken out of the ground 36 years after he was buried. His body was moved to a new tomb. And it was still preserved!

MUMMY MAP

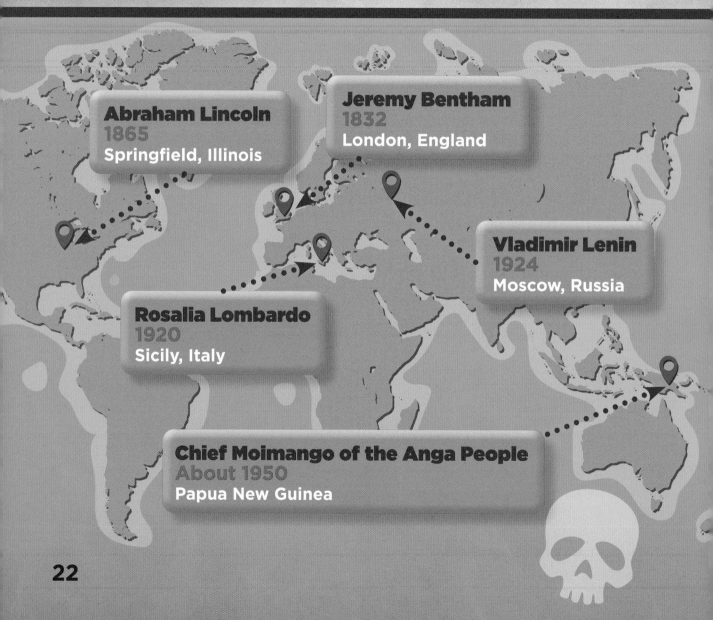

Abraham Lincoln
1865
Springfield, Illinois

Jeremy Bentham
1832
London, England

Vladimir Lenin
1924
Moscow, Russia

Rosalia Lombardo
1920
Sicily, Italy

Chief Moimango of the Anga People
About 1950
Papua New Guinea

GLOSSARY

artificial (ahr-tuh-FISH-uhl) **made or done by human beings**

bacteria (bak-TEER-ee-uh) **tiny life-forms that can only be seen with a microscope**

catacombs (KAT-uh-kohmz) **underground cemeteries made up of tunnels and rooms**

chemicals (KEM-uh-kuhlz) **natural or human-made substances**

embalmer (em-BAHM-ur) **a person who preserves dead bodies**

eternity (ih-TUR-nih-tee) **an unending period of time**

flesh (FLESH) **the soft part of a body that covers the bones**

lifelike (LIFE-like) **looking alive or real**

memorial (muh-MOR-ee-uhl) **something that is created to remember and honor a person or an event**

monks (MUHNGKS) **men who have devoted their lives to God and are part of a religious community**

overcome (oh-vur-KUHM) **to be strongly affected by an event**

philosopher (fuh-LAH-suh-fur) **a person who thinks and writes about the meaning of life**

preserve (prih-ZURV) **to protect something so that it stays in its original state**

revolution (rev-uh-LOO-shuhn) **the overthrow of a government to bring about a new system**

skeleton (SKEL-uh-tuhn) **the bones of a person or animal**

tomb (TOOM) **a grave, room, or building for holding a dead body**

toxic (TOK-sik) **poisonous**

tradition (truh-DISH-uhn) **a belief, idea, or custom that is handed down from generation to generation**

FIND OUT MORE

Books

Carney, Elizabeth. *Mummies*. Washington, D.C.: National Geographic, 2009.

Nobleman, Marc Tyler. *Mummies*. Mankato, MN: Heinemann-Raintree, 2006.

Sloan, Christopher. *Mummies*. Washington, D.C.: National Geographic, 2010.

Websites

Encyclopedia Britannica: What Is Jeremy Bentham's "Auto-Icon"?
https://www.britannica.com/story/what-is-jeremy-benthams-auto-icon

NOVA: 10 Ways to Make a Mummy
https://www.pbs.org/wgbh/nova/ancient/10-ways-mummy.html

Palermo Catacombs: The Capuchin Catacombs
http://www.palermocatacombs.com

INDEX

ABOUT THE AUTHOR

Joyce Markovics digs mummies—and all kinds of curious things. She also loves learning about people from the past and telling their stories.